A TRIP THROUGH

NORTHERN AND CENTRAL

FLORIDA,

During March and April, 1882.

By FRANK SIMPSON.

EAST ORANGE, N. J.:
East Orange Gazette Print,
1882.

Northern and Central Florida.

———❖—

One Thursday evening about the middle of March, Hon. L. M. Lawson and wife, together with myself, left New York for Jacksonville. The next morning reaching Washington, our party was increased by other gentlemen, all of whom were on their way to Jacksonville to attend a directors' meeting of the Florida Central and Western Railroad, and I had been kindly invited to join the party in a trip over the road, which they intended to make when the meeting was finished.

After a warm and dusty ride, we reached Jacksonville Saturday evening at about half-past five, the train by some accident happening to be on time. During our stay in this city we stopped at the Windsor Hotel, finding it to be a first-class house in every respect. Before I had been long in the Land of Flowers I found that my knowledge of the State amounted almost to nothing, and that those impressions which I had had all my life were now to be entirely forgotten. Florida is often imagined as a country, and perhaps a swampy one, too, lying somewhere down South, which will do very well for invalids and consumptives, but which is no place for a strong, enterprising man. This impression is, however, totally wrong. As for swamps, they are rarely found. Even the famous Everglade Region, which appears to many one vast mud-hole, is but a prairie-like region, dotted with islands which are covered with cypress, oak, cedar, pine and other such trees, while around these islands is a pure, clear water varying in depth from three to thirty inches. Should the attempt which is now being made to drain this country be successful, millions of acres of the finest sugar and cotton lands in the world will be but forests are now employed in the cultivation of vegetables for our northern markets. Frosts do now and then, however, come to this portion of the State, as happened during the winter of 1880–1, when all of the orange trees were killed off. A new growth has been set out, but here the orange is not so profitable, owing to its northern situation. This part of Florida is best fitted for live stock and crops, and in no place do they flourish better. All northern fruits and vegetables, together with the hardier of the southern, grow here with less care than has to be expended upon them in either the North or West. The country in the northwestern part of Florida is rolling and to a northern eye has a most homelike appearance.

The lumber trade is a profitable one, those mills which are already established paying well, while new ones are constantly springing up. Indeed, in more cases than one a town has been built, which, in the first place, owed its foundation to the establishment of a saw mill. A most interesting and well attested fact concerning the pine forests of Florida is, that whereas in other countries, when the original trees are cut down, a growth of scrub oak or some other inferior kind of wood springs up, yet in this State the original forest is succeeded by a new growth of equally good pine, which is large enough for commercial use in fifteen or twenty years. This new growth happens not once, but continually, and renders the pine forests of Florida literally inexhaustible.

In the evening at about five o'clock we reached Tallahassee, the capital of the State. Leaving our valises at the hotel, we were instantly taken for a drive around the city and out into the country, and so had an opportunity to judge of its merits before nightfall. The city possesses about twenty-five hundred inhabitants and is a most charming place. It is situated a little above the surrounding country, and a view from the roof of the State House shows a beautiful prospect of rolling hills, farms, clumps of trees, forest land, valleys and brooks. Tallahassee has good roads, beautiful drives, and a most delightful atmosphere. The society here is perhaps the best in the State, the people being hospitable and friendly and devoted to the cultivation of flowers. Once a year, during the month of March, the inhabitants hold a floral exhibition, when the wealth and beauty of the flowers displayed does great honor to the tastes of the exhibitors.

Within seven miles of the city is Lake Jackson, an irregular but beautiful sheet of water, situated among the hills, and said by our driver to be fifteen miles in length. The shores of the lake afford beautiful sites for villas, which are, as yet, being built only to a very small extent. A new hotel, which by the way is very much needed, is now being built at Tallahassee, and this, with the other attractions possessed by the city, should make it a place of popular resort for northern visitors.

Chattahoochee, situated on the Appalachicola river, some forty miles distant from the capital, was also visited by us. The place consists of nothing but the railroad depot, steamboat landing, two or three huts and a building which we supposed to be a hotel.

We left Tallahassee Wednesday evening, and after a comfortable night's rest on the train, reached Jacksonville in the morning. Here resting a day, we again left on Friday morning for Cedar Keys. Our direction now led us across the State to the southwest, running at first over the Florida Transit Railroad, which reaches from Fernandina to Cedar Keys ; then afterwards leaving the Transit road at Waldo, we entered upon that called the Peninsular, which stretches to Ocala. The managers of these two roads are now constructing, and have partly finished, lines to Tampa on the west coast of Florida, and to the Indian River region on the east coast. These extended roads will supply a long felt want in the State, and will open up lands which for fertility are excelled by none in Florida.

Our route now lay through a region more tropical and consequently presenting many new points of interest. The woods were far more luxuriant, the ground being thickly grown with all sorts of shrubs, long grasses and bushes, and in looking back over the road which we had just passed there appeared a long vista of green, growing close up to the track and tapering away almost to a point.

Cedar Keys, the terminus of the Florida Transit Railroad, is situated on the Gulf of Mexico and is a quiet, thrifty town. Here are found the best oysters in Florida. They are shipped

to all parts of the State, to all the large southern cities, and
even to places as far north as Louisville. To one, however,
who has been accustomed to the luxury of Blue Points and
Rockaways, their taste is, to say the least, insipid, and perhaps
the less said about them the better.

Faber has a manufactory here for the making of cedar pen-
holders and pencils. Much of the work is done by women,
who earn from twelve to eighteen dollars per month, according to their expertness. Cedar Keys has a tropical appearance and seems to remind one that at one time Florida was
under the government of a different nation from that which
now rules it. Large quantities of cedar are shipped north
every year from this place, and the trade of the town, which
is mostly wholesale, amounts annually to several hundred
thousand dollars.

Leaving Cedar Keys the same evening, we returned over
the Transit road to Waldo, where our car switched off on the
Peninsular road, which leads to Ocala. This city is the capital
of Marion county and has a population of a little over a thousand. The soil here is excellent, and a drive into the country
around Ocala shows immense fields of banana and orange
trees, while the people are not behind in the cultivation of
winter vegetables. Marion county has a population of about
fifteen thousand and not a bank within its limits.

At about half-past eight we left Ocala, having as usual our
special train in waiting for us, and after a ride of about six
miles reached Silver Springs, where commenced a day of
beauty such as I never saw before, and fear I shall never see
again. Nothing which I ever saw in Europe, not even in far-
famed Italy, could compare for beauty with what I viewed that
day. How my trip down the Ock-la-wa-ha river impressed me,
and what I saw, I shall endeavor to portray, but like as I was
taught in early days that beauty itself is incapable of analysis,
so now I find it incapable of description.

Silver Springs, the beginning of the trip, is a large basin of
water covering an area of about three acres, while the depth
is that of sixty-five or seventy feet. Here is the landing of
one of the strangest little steamers ever seen. Ours, the
Osceola, was two stories high, the lower one being quite low,

while the upper story contained the dining room and some half dozen little state-rooms, with a small deck in front from which to view the scenery. Above this second deck, near the edge of the roof, stands the pilot-house, while the little steamer itself is propelled by a stern wheel, and such are the turnings and twistings of the journey that two rudders are required to steer the little craft. These are parallel to each other, in the stern, and when the helm is put "hard" either one way or the other, the boat is almost completely stopped, while the rear seems to be flying around one way and the bow the other.

The surprise and pleasure of the journey commences the very instant you board the steamer. On looking down we began to wonder how the boat ever got where she was, for what we saw below us was certainly land, only it was a thousand times more beautiful than any we had ever seen before. Soon, however, we began to perceive that the Osceola was not ashore, but that in gazing downward we were looking through at least fifty feet of water, and that the land which appeared so beautiful was that at the bottom of the spring. Presently the steamer commenced a series of diminutive puffs and was soon in the middle of the spring, while with eyes still cast down we saw every stone and pebble through an essence of clearness seventy feet deep. Fom the bow of the vessel the waves rolled off, curling into crystal and green, and every drop sparkled and shone like small globes of transparent white.

From the Silver Spring itself the steamer enters what is known as Silver Spring Run, a narrow stream which leads to the Ock-la-wa-ha River proper. During these nine miles which separate you from the river the water is as clear as that in the fountain head. Nothing in the river nor upon its bed escapes the eye. The moss and grass upon the bottom are plainly discernible, waving to and fro, sometimes seeming to beckon you to share with them that purity and beauty which they enjoy, while with their blades glistening below in the sunlight, now shining and now disappearing, they seem to tell you that they possess that secret by which they may turn everything they touch into gold. Again, stone appears beneath, which looks like molten silver, while here and there, now hiding among the moss, and now laughing at you from the river's bed, lie objects sparkling like large diamonds and defying you to reach them. Over such treasures swim the fish, every motion visible, proceeding now in schools and now again wandering alone, as if tired of company and wishing to enjoy the beautiful waters in solitude. Suddenly a large turtle comes into view, swimming as fast as his short legs will carry him toward the shore or some friendly rock. Even he, this turtle, is to be envied, for while he shows to greedy mortals only his black shell, yet should a glance be obtained at the inside as he strikes out, it will be seen that his coat is lined with shining silver. Every object in this limpid crystal is transformed and takes to itself new forms and new colors befitting its heavenly abode. And still, as the steamer passes on the water continually changes its color, taking the hues of the objects over which it flows, changing from a dark green to a light, then becoming almost black, turning again to silver, then to brown, and presenting each moment some new and beautiful tint.

But while I had been thus proceeding for miles with eyes cast down I looked up, only to discover that like the old man in " The Pilgrim's Progress," I had been living with my eyes upon the ground in search of that treasure which was rather to be found by looking above. When you gaze around you wonder if you have not left this world and entered Fairyland. Surely such a sight was never seen before. I thought of that picture which represented Youth sailing down the River of Life, but of the two I felt that I should choose the Ock-la-wa-ha.

Now it no longer seems strange that the Indians called the stream by their beautiful name, which means Crooked Waters. Often the distance of only a few rods in front can be seen, while to tell whether the steamer turns to the right or left is impossible. Within the space of five minutes her bow may have pointed to all points of the compass, north, south, east and west. Away goes the little boat around one bend only to enter upon another curving around in the opposite direction. Sometimes the curves are so short that first the steamer runs her bow upon the shore in front of her, then, having been headed down stream again by a negro who handles a long pole, she dashes across the river, almost knocking down a tree on that side, only to rush back again upon the other bank, while almost before she is fairly in the channel another bend is commenced almost as sharp as the first. All day long you are dodging around among the trees, ducking your head every few moments to avoid the branches and wondering what you are going to strike next.

But while we had been thus twisting and turning in all directions, and while we had been plucking the leaves and flowers from the trees as we passed, the lovely appearance of the forest through which the river flowed had not escaped our notice. This stream differs from almost all others, in as much as it has nothing which might be called its banks. The trees, immense cypress, oaks, gums, maples and magnolias, with other varieties, seem to have sprung up in the river itself, while the stream appears to have worn a path through the very forest. Here every tree and shrub grows in the most luxuriant profusion. The cypress appears everywhere, suspending from its branches the beautiful silver-gray Spanish moss, which appears when hanging motionless like long tresses of hair, but when swaying in the wind seems to be the long slender arms of some water spirit inviting your approach ; or again a snake-like tongue, writhing and twisting as if in pain. Trees encircled here and there with bands of bright red bark and bearing berries as bright and as red ; flowers of all colors and shapes ; leaves with the beautiful tints of a northern autumn ; palmettoes stretching high into the air their long slender trunks, topped with a ball of gracefully curving leaves ; great forest giants side by side with the young cypress just appearing, all interlaced and tangled in a luxuriance known only in a tropical country, lined the shores without intermission : while the water, trees, flowers, mosses, everything seemed to melt into each other in such a liquid beauty that it was impossible to tell whether we were looking at the woods or at the water, or whether we saw neither and were only dreaming.

As these never tiring beauties pass before the eye, suddenly a water turkey with long legs and still longer neck rises from the stream, and flying off with a discordant cry, perches itself

upon the limb of some lofty tree to await the steamer's approach, or again he may swim before you, diving out of sight
for minutes together and then raising his snake-like neck above
the surface, he darts it here and there and everywhere, turning
it in all directions with lightning-like rapidity, suddenly to
disappear again under the water ; perhaps he may rise again,
having secured his prey, or he may be lost sight of altogether.
Now moccasins are seen coiled up asleep upon some log ; perhaps not even to awake unless disturbed by the long pole of
the darky in the bow, while alligators continually present
themselves for public inspection. Sometimes they are found
lying asleep upon some log or the shore, not disappearing
until the steamer is almost abreast with them, when, diving
into the river, they make their way into the woods. Again in
the grass ahead a dark body is seen which suddenly disappears,
and beneath the water may be seen an alligator endeavoring
to hide, while anon a splash can be heard, the disturbance of
the water seen, and no more. By the time the journey is half
over, and especially if the day is a warm one, so many of this
tribe will have been seen, and so many others imagined, that
the cry of "alligator, ho !" will hardly awaken any enthusiasm.

The alligator, owing to the raid which is now being made
upon it, is slowly disappearing from Central Florida. An
order has been received from a St. Louis firm for five thousand
hides to be delivered by the fall, while some firm in the
Eastern States has been promised three thousand more by the
same time. Hundreds are also taken North every year by
visitors. While on one line of steamers up the Ock-la-wa-ha,
people who have lived in the city all their lives, and have
never handled a gun before, are allowed to bang away all day
over your head and by your ears at every defenceless alligator
which comes into view. This slaughter of the animal for no
purpose whatever, except to gratify the brutal whim of some
would-be sportsman, should be prohibited ; and it is to be
hoped that this second line of steamers will follow the good
example of the first, and cause those brave shots to save their
skill for a more useful purpose.

About two o'clock in the day the cypress gates are reached.
These are two very large trees standing opposite each other

on either side of the stream, so close that your further progress seems debarred. Through these gates you view for
some distance almost the narrowest part of the river. You
wonder how the steamer will ever get through the opening,
and then you want to know where she will find water enough
to float after she is through. Nevertheless the little boat runs
her bow between the trees, and after striking first one and
then the other, has passed the gates, and then for some distance threads her way among the trees in a manner quite
wonderful.

Along the sides of the river appear frequently delightful
little inlets, meandering away into the forest, while little
streams wend their way, soon to hide their pure bosoms with
a veil of vines, leaves and flowers. Again, another softly
glides into view, coming forth quietly and sadly, seeming
either reluctant or bashful to leave its home of the cypress
and the oak, while even now, as the wind blows, these trees
may be heard to mourn and sigh over their loss.

Thus all day long new beauties and new points of interest
continually present themselves, while the eye never tires of
gazing at the wealth of tree, vine, and flower, which are
beautiful as they can be only in a tropical clime.

But if the day is thus charming, what can be said of the
night ? Now a scene is presented which baffles description.
As the day begins to fade and the pilot can no longer see his
way, a large bright fire of pine knots is lighted above the pilot
house in an iron basin. Instantly every form and color becomes new and strange. Directly in front Night itself is
brooding upon the river. Darkness is there veiling every
object in mystery, and now and then as the fire of pine knots
grows brighter and again fades, strange forms wax and wane,
flit to and fro in the distance, and then disappear. Again they
come into view, when, perhaps, one takes shape and allows you
to approach it. Nearer and nearer it comes, when a grim
monster towers into the sky, stretching on all sides long bony
arms covered with a light drapery which hangs as if torn into
a thousand shreds. As you gaze, first one and then another
appears, until they almost block the vessel's way, shaking, as

a breeze stirs them, their tattered garments, and threatening vengeance for this nightly disturbance. Nearer and nearer they come. Gradually each form loses its monster shape as the steamer approaches. Their long, thin arms fade into limbs of trees, every leaf of which glitters like a blade of frosted silver, while each shred of their tattered garments becomes a tress of silver-gray moss, changed now to a tress of bronze. Again and again these forms, at first strange and weird, loom out from the darkness, only to melt as they come nearer into forms of rarest beauty.

In the inky river below, the leaves of the water lily, as they appear and disappear beneath the tiny waves, have become silver and gold, while every drop of water running over their surface sparkles from its background of black and gold as never diamonds shone. Trees along the banks whose trunks during the day were merely white, become now pillars of white, glistening fire. Every tree, leaf, vine, or flower takes to itself new forms and colors such as the day never imagined.

As you follow with the eye some object which is passing, the bright colors begin to fade, the pillars of fire lose their brightness, trees and moss again assume their ghostly shape, the leaves of the water-lily are no longer silver and gold, while the bright drops of water have become as black as the river. Above all, as if waving a fiery farewell, fly the sparks from the fire of pine knots. The little steamer puffs on and on while still appear, grow distinct, and fade again the figures of such a night as can never be forgotten—so strange, weird, awful, and yet so beautiful.

Once during the night the whistle of the steamer was blown. Instantly there arose on all sides dismal cries and shrieks from each long-legged bird, many of which flew off, loudly flapping their wings and seeming to curse that which had disturbed their peace. These, too, died away, and soon the woods were as still and lonely as before.

Our little steamer arrived at Palatka, on the St. Johns River at about one o'clock in the morning, but not wishing to go ashore at that unseemly hour, we took possession of the state-rooms, and spent the night on board. Our breakfast was taken at the Putnam House, one of the best hotels in Florida. It is very nicely furnished, is cool, roomy, and presents an excellent table.

Palatka is a very pretty city, beautifully situated on ground rising slightly from the river, and has a population of about eight hundred, who are mostly Northern people. Its streets are wide and generally shaded with orange trees. The small boy, however, has but very little incentive to " hook " the fruit, as he would call it, as it is sour. The city appears enterprising and growing. The soil thereabouts is rich and productive, and from here also large quantities of vegetables are shipped yearly to the North. In this vicinity also are many orange groves, that of Colonel Hart, situated across the river, being one of the most famous in the State.

Palatka shows evidences of improvement and thrift, while one of the most pleasant sights to a Northern visitor is the grass which fills the yards and even lines the sides of the roads. Many cities in Florida which are really thriving, go-ahead places, have an air of desolation and neglect for want of this very grass. The people seem to care little or nothing for its cultivation, and in the towns where the soil is often sandy, care is needed to induce it to grow.

Having made a tour of the city, and visited its store of Floridian curiosities, most of which are made in the North, we left Palatka on the steamer St. Johns, on our way down the river. This fine boat is remembered by many as one which used to ply in the summer between New York and Long Branch, returning to Florida in the winter. Trade, however, has increased here to such an extent during the past few years, that if New Yorkers wish to take a sail on the Steamer St. Johns they will have to visit Florida, as she has left the North forever.

The river itself, during its first ninety-six miles, is a fine large stream, varying from one to six miles in width, is deep, and has a slow current. Here the shores are covered with extensive forests, and lined frequently with pretty and attractive little towns.

About We-la-ka, however, the stream changes in appearance, becomes narrower and very crooked. The shores are flat and covered with a dense growth of trees, great vines, and a jungle of tropical grasses, brambles and bushes. This continues, with the exception now and then of pine or high soil clearings, to Lake Monroe, about eighty miles distant. The shore being flat, the river frequently widens out into small lakes, where game and fish are found in great abundance. Alligators in this region avoid the steamer, disappearing whenever it comes into sight, remembering two well that their lives are not safe from the gun of the sporting fiend. Beautiful flowers are found everywhere, while birds of brilliant plumage enliven the scene.

Above Lake Monroe to Lake Washington, the source of the St. Johns, the river becomes very crooked, narrow, and shallow. The distance is two hundred and fourteen miles, and the stream winds through a vast prairie-like region, where trees are seen but seldom. This part of Florida excels for grazing ; vast herds of cattle are seen upon every side, while all sorts of game and fish abound.

The mouth of the St. Johns is obstructed by a bar which, at the present time, leaves only ten or twelve feet of water at high tide. About one hundred and fifty thousand dollars have already been expended upon a system of jetties in order to deepen the channel. Florida desires an appropriation from Congress of three millions, with which amount they believe the channel could be made twenty feet at high water. This, of course, would be of great advantage to Jacksonville, as it would open her port to vessels double the draught of those which can now enter. The name given the river by the Indians was that of Wa-la-ka, to which two meanings are assigned. The one signifies " It has its own way ;" the other, "a chain of lakes." The latter translation seems to me the more appropriate, but as both are given, each may choose for himself.

Our first place of departure from the river took place at Tocoi, eighteen miles below Palatka. Here are only the steamboat landing and railroad depot, from which cars run to St. Augustine. The distance is fourteen miles over a flat and uninteresting country, covered mostly with pine.

St. Augustine itself, however, is well worth a visit. The

oldest town in the United States, it was founded by the Spaniards under Menendez in 1565, and still retains much of its old Spanish appearance. The streets are narrow and very straight for an old city. There are no regularly constructed sidewalks, the doors of the houses opening upon the street itself. Many of the houses are built of coquina, a rock formed of shells, which, although by no means a hard stone, yet is very durable. In many places the houses project over the street, forming a shelter for the passengers beneath, which, before the time of umbrellas, must have been very acceptable. But besides the foreign appearance of the streets, St. Augustine has other sights, and those too which are worth visiting.

Fronting the Plaza de la Constitucion, is the old cathedral, which was built in 1793, while one of its bells bears the date 1682. There is very little ornamentation discernible, either inside or out of the building, the principal object of attraction being the Moorish belfry. The cathedral seems to feel its weight of years, and looks much older than it really is. Some enterprising Americans, the younger generation no doubt, have conceived the highly civilized idea of repairing the old building. By this I judged from what an old citizen told me, that they desired to remove whatever was old about the church, and replace it with something new and handsome, something befitting, perhaps, their refined and modernized tastes. But said the old man, who was a communicant there : "They shall never touch it while we old people are alive. They may repair it when we are dead and gone, but not while we live and can prevent it." The old gentleman was right, and whoever should venture to remove one stone of the old cathedral until safety demands it, should be branded as worse than a barbarian.

The old gates of St. Augustine are interesting, but the wall through which they were formerly the entrance no longer exists. The towers and sentry boxes, although hardly imposing, are very picturesque and ancient looking, reminding one of the time of knights and squires, lords and ladies.

The most interesting sight in St. Augustine, is Fort Marion. This most picturesque old structure, with its deep, broad moat, towers, massive walls, and dungeons, was completed in 1756, having occupied one hundred and sixty-four years in its construction. It was entirely built by negro slaves, Indians, and prisoners of war, and is constructed of coquina rock, quarried on Anastasia Island. While held by the British it was said to be the prettiest fort in the King's dominions. It is of no use, however, in modern warfare, and is gradually crumbling to decay. The old fort is a romantic spot, and is much frequented by young married couples, lovers, and those who are either desirous of entering that blissful state, or by those who, having entered, are desirous to continue therein.

The old sea wall, four feet wide, built of coquina and granite, is nearly a mile in length and protects almost the entire river front of the city. Just why it was built I have been unable to discover, as St. Augustine, being situated on the Matanzas river, which is separated from the ocean by Anastasia Island, is never subjected to any storms upon the shore of the city itself. It is an ornament, but, I should think, an expensive one.

The Plaza de la Constitucion is an interesting old square, situated about the center of the city, and with its two monuments and old market place, now in disuse, adds not only a charm to the city, but also serves to increase that foreign and ancient appearance, which is the chief feature of St. Augustine. This city is considered among the most healthy in Florida. Malaria is almost unknown, while frosts seldom occur, the average temperature during the winter being 58 degrees.

Again leaving St. Augustine, at 8.45, A. M., we took the little railroad to Tocoi, where we boarded the steamer for Jacksonville, and after a very pleasant ride of forty-three miles, reached our destination at about two o'clock. Here resting a day, we were hurried off the next morning for Fernandina, having to do our packing, eat our breakfast, and reach the depot inside of forty minutes. The ride from Jacksonville to Fernandina, a distance of thirty-two miles, is very pleasant, passing through some densely wooded and very pretty country.

Fernandina is a very pretty city, situated on Amelia Island, close to the boundary line between Georgia and Florida, and having a population of about two thousand. Its harbor is by far the best in the State, and a system of jetties is now in course of construction, which will open this port to steamers of the very largest size. The city is the terminus of the two principal railroads in Florida, the Florida Central and Western, reaching to Tallahassee, and the Florida Transit, extending to Cedar Keys ; a short line also connects it directly with Jacksonville, while all natural advantages seem to make it the port through which Florida must ship all her products.

While in Fernandina we were courteously invited by ex-Senator Yulee, to accompany him on a tour around the harbor. We gladly accepted the invitation, and at about ten o'clock in the morning, boarded a private tug, when, assisted by the Senator's store of valuable information, we had an opportunity to view the finest harbor south of the Chesapeake. We passed old Fort Clinch, long since abandoned, and crossed over to Cumberland Island, on which stands " Dungeness;" the former home of Gen. Nathaniel Green, one of our revolutionary heroes. This charming and magnificent home was burned during the early part of the civil war, and is now a massive old ruin. In a graveyard near by, is buried Harry Lee, known as " Light House Harry," the father of Gen. Robert E. Lee. While on our tug, we had a chance to view the fine bay, large, and deep enough to hold the fleets of the world. Arriving again at the pier, we drove down to the famous Amelia Island Beach, one of the finest in America. Here for twenty miles this drive extends along the edge of the ocean over a white, hard, and smooth sand. There is an hotel on the beach, which is frequented during the summer by native Floridians, and it is rather strange that this place is not more popular among health seekers, for, while it possesses all the inducements of a northern resort, it has the advantage of being in a southern climate.

The city of Fernandina has grown but little during a number of years past, owing to the fact that most of the property had been seized by the Government during the war, for non-payment of taxes. This has, however, lately been restored to the rightful owners, and now being free from all entanglement, the city will doubtless commence a rapid growth. It is

undoubtedly the port of Florida. It has direct railroad com-
munication with every part of the State, and commerce with
Liverpool, New York, Charleston, Savannah, and other
Southern cities. Vessels which will probably never be able to
reach Jacksonville, have free access to Fernandina, while time
can be saved by shipping from this port. The city has a fine
situation, and is very healthy and cool, the sea sending the
most delightful breeze over the Island during the whole day.
From its natural advantages Fernandina was meant to be the
principal city in Florida, and I should not be surprised to find
that in fifty years it had taken the lead from Jacksonville.

From the roof of the Egmont House, one of the best
hotels in Florida, is a view which is beautiful at every hour,
but especially at sunset. In the west flows the Amelia river,
which as the sun goes down assumes the most rich and gor-
geous colors. Streaks of dark purple, which grow darker and
richer as the light wanes, cover the river, while shades of gold
and red lie between, each melting into the other with rarest
tint. Beyond, with strips of dark land between, are two rib-
bons of gold, which taper away towards the left into points,
and then disappear. As darkness comes on, the purple alone
remains, which supports upon its royal bosom ships, the
masts and rigging of which are clearly defined against the
sky, while so peaceful and tranquil is the scene that Quiet
itself seems to have chosen that place for its home. In the
east can be seen the ocean rolling its line of white upon the
beach, and to the north, rising from a grove of trees, stands
the white lighthouse, whose beacon ever fades and again
grows bright. Around and below is the city, with its wealth
of trees and houses, from whose windows appear one by one
the lights, varying in brightness as the houses are near or far.
Then off in the distance are the woods fading away into the
darkness, while the whole scene is so quiet and tranquil that
it seems a pity morning should ever come.

In Fernandina, called the Newport of the South, we remained almost three days, and on our return to Jacksonville
our tour in Florida was virtually at an end. We remained in
this city, however, for some days longer, and each day as I

learned more and more of the State, my belief in its future greatness became more and more strengthened.

So situated is this State, and such are its natural advantages, that the wants of every one seem here to meet their fulfillment. For the invalid there is perpetual summer, no cold blasts of the North to congeal the very blood in his veins, and to extinguish the little life which there is left. A genial climate gives out-door exercise from January to December, while I can assert, both from my own observation and also upon the authority of others, that many arriving in Florida almost dead have now not only recovered their health, but are on their way to fortune, owning orange groves or farms, holding positions of trust, and otherwise benefitting both themselves and the country, and having before them the prospect of a long and happy life. This result, however, is not to be accomplished by going to Jacksonville, shutting oneself in a hot and dark room, and then as soon as the warm weather of March comes, running away to the North, expecting to fine summer there. Health and strength are gained by care, such as would be used at home, and by making use of the pure air, light and sun, which God has so bountifully given.

Florida is, however, not a land for invalids only. The farmer and immigrant are offered advantages here which far surpass any to be found in Kansas or Nebraska. There is not a northern or semi-tropical fruit, vegetable or grain which does not grow in Florida, and grow well, while the care needed to produce a successful crop is much less than that which has to be expended in any other portion of the Union. The choicest fruits and vegetables can be placed in the northern market at a time when their value is enormous. Strawberries, tomatoes, green peas, cucumbers, and similar productions, can be brought to perfection long before their seed is even sown in the North, and the prices obtained for these luxuries render the profits fabulous.

During the winter of 1880–1, the most severe ever known in Florida, a country fair was held on February 22, in Sanford, Orange county, for the purpose of displaying their winter productions. The results obtained seem almost incredible, but in order to show what Florida can produce in mid-winter, I shall quote a few sentences from a report prepared by Dr. J. L. Richardson for the Mount Sterling (Kentucky) *Democrat.* He says : " There were turnips measuring three feet in circumference ; cabbages weighing from twelve to fifteen pounds, and radishes as much as nine pounds, solid and brittle. The *Rean Luxurians,* or Te-o-sin-te—grass of the gods —exhibited by Dr. Kenworthy, is eight or nine feet long, and resembles corn fodder, and is said to be very prolific, yielding from fifty to one hundred tons per acre. Heads of lettuce that would cover a dinner, plate looked fresh and crisp; while onions, leeks, kale, parsnips, etc., lay around in rich profusion. Potatoes planted on Christmas day were of fine size for table use, and altogether it would be difficult to imagine a more splendid and attractive show of garden vegetables, maturing in the open garden, while all the other States lay congealed in the icy chains of winter."

The foregoing is a part of Dr. Richardson's report in relation to winter vegetables, and as to other Florida products the result may seem equally astounding. An orange grove will bear in three years from planting, and in five years will be self-supporting. From this time it rapidly advances, paying at first hundreds, then soon thousands of dollars per acre ; while from the same amount of ground, from four to six thousand dollars have been realized. Bananas pay from twelve hundred to two thousand dollars ; pine-apples from eight hundred to twelve hundred dollars. Sugar cane grows to the height of twelve or sixteen feet, single stalks producing more than a gallon of juice, and from five to six hundred gallons of syrup per acre. The same roots will produce new stalks for several years, unless injured by cold, drought, or excess of rain. As many as nineteen crops from the same roots have been raised in the Indian River region ; while on the shores of Lake Worth there is now growing cane which has not been replanted since the Indian wars, which ended in 1842. A planter on the Indian River netted, with the help of one negro man, sixteen hundred dollars from five acres, while other results equally good have been obtained, of which this is merely an example.

Cotton of the best grade is raised here, averaging from one hundred and fifty to two hundred pounds per acre ; though this yield is often doubled. This crop is safer here than in any other State. Corn is, all things considered, one of the most profitable crops in Florida, for although at first producing less per acre than can be grown in the West, yet when all expenses incidental to such a crop are considered, the raising of corn becomes very lucrative. The above mentioned are a few examples of the many and various crops produced in this State. In the case of a few products, the yield may be less per acre than is grown in other parts of the Union, but when other advantages are weighed, as the price of land ; the seasons which always give two crops, sometimes three and possibly four ; the cost of gathering, housing and similar outlays; I think it may be safely said that here the profits are much greater, and the danger of failure much less than in any other State.

Florida, as has been truly said, is rapidly becoming a Northern colony. Year by year the number from New England, the Middle States, and the Northwest, is steadily increasing. This element, although by no means the largest, is yet by far the most important, and to it is due all that prosperity which is now spreading over every portion of the State. Railroad and steamboat lines, the largest farms and orange groves, the finest houses and grounds, the great saw mills and hotels, are all for the most part owned by Northern men ; while those cities are the most thrifty which contain the largest number of this hardy and energetic people. The immigrants to this State are unusually intelligent, understanding how to read and write, and having an appreciation of the truth that wealth lies in the steady and diligent cultivation of the soil, none expecting, as is often the case in the far West, to make a fortune in a day. These people almost invariably succeed ; and, after a few years of steady toil, are repaid by finding themselves not only well-to-do in the world, but also by becoming, thanks partly to their own labor, an important member of what is now perhaps a thriving young community.

There are also found here Northern people of another class, who come not so much to make a fortune as to enjoy that which they have already made. In and around Jacksonville are found many such, while the banks of the St. Johns contain many villas, which are inhabited during the winter by the Northern gentleman. In the above mentioned city, among many others, is General Spinner, while somewhat higher up upon the bank of the river may be seen the residence of Mrs. Harriet Beecher Stowe.

As a second class of those who inhabit Florida may be mentioned the old Southern families, those of the old regime, who before the war owned their slaves, lived in princely style, and now, for the most part, inhabit the northwestern part of the State. These families are hospitable and kind, courteous and polite to the highest degree, but nevertheless live, as far as circumstances will allow, in the old way, and even yet are slow to adopt those new customs and opinions which have pervaded the country since the war. A northern stranger or immigrant will be always kindly treated, even assisted and cared for if in need, but he is always, to a certain extent, regarded as an interloper. These old families are gradually passing away, and with them the remembrance of those wrongs, deep and real as they are, is also gradually disappearing. The younger generation is growing up imbued with the spirit and ideas of to-day. They naturally grow with the times, become more energetic, and soon no doubt this northwestern portion of the State will become, as from its appearance it well deserves to be, Northern, if not in reality, at least in enterprise and growth.

The negro constitutes the third, the largest, but the most unimportant class in the State. Numbering almost half the population of all Florida, and living in the climate for which he seems especially made, he is, nevertheless, as a trustworthy laborer, of but little advantage. He is docile and good natured, but is still very untrustworthy, requiring constant watching in order to exact from him his daily work. The best negro is he who has the blackest face. He is more steady going, anxious to please, and willing to execute, as far as he is able, those orders received from his overseer. Negroes of a lighter color, mulattoes, and other such, are often insolent, frequently addicted to drink and gambling, and, upon the whole, are of far less value as laborers than their blacker brothers. The negro in Florida is slowly, and will doubtless eventually be altogether, displaced as a workman by the foreign element, which latter class, although small, is unusually thrifty and industrious in this State, the Irish being hardly found.

The fourth and perhaps the most interesting class of inhabitants is the "cracker." Just what he is, and where he came from, nobody seems to know. He lives in the woods away from all settlements, and as civilization and population increase, is driven further and further away, until finally, it is to be hoped, he will be crowded out into the sea and drowned. He is an interesting study, for his characteristics are many and various. Lazy, ignorant, squalid and mean, he is at the same time vindictive and stupid. His appearance is tall and gaunt, his hair dirty and matted, having staring eyes and a slouching gait. His house is a log cabin, usually having but one room and no floor. Here he lives in dirt and squalor, his wife as bad as himself, and both subsisting on cabbage palmettoes, sweet potatoes and wild fruits, with pellets of clay as a condiment. Now and then the "cracker" gives a ball, inviting his friends for miles around, and after assembling in his hut, they commence their dance, which often lasts two or three days, and subsequently ends up in a brawl, when the best man carries off the lady.

This State is often represented as one in which malaria is found in every part, and to the danger of which every one is more or less subjected. This statement is wholly untrue. To assert that no cases of this disease were ever known in Florida would be about as worthy of belief as to assert that no cases were ever known North. Those troubles and derangements which northern people sometimes suffer in Florida, and which they attribute to malaria, are the results of their own imprudence, to over-eating, over-exertion, exclusion of fresh air, and to the taking of medicines intended to ward off a disease which exists only in their imagination. Dr. Joseph P. Logan, of Atlanta, says, that since 1844 he has navigated, at different times, the various streams of the State, including Lake Okeechobee and the Everglades, has slept for two monhts in an open boat with no covering but an awning stretched above him, and that at no time did either he or his companions suffer from malaria or a chill. One hears most of this bug-bear from the agents of certain hotels, steamboat lines, and the like, who endeavor by their stories of malaria, to frighten travelers from one part of the State and induce him to take up their abode in another, or to travel over lines in which they themselves are interested. Colonel Hart, who has lived for years upon the banks of the St. Johns, and who owns a line of steamers which traverse the Ock-la-wa-ha, and who would certainly be well acquainted with cases, if such there were, has informed me that in this very district, which most people would consider especially productive of malaria, cases of this trouble are unknown. Let those who visit Florida avoid excess in what they eat and drink, beware of undue exposure, breathe the pure air night and day, and they will find that Florida contains no more of this disease than do the Northern States.

In conclusion, perhaps, a few words in regard to the price of Florida lands would not be inappropriate. Farms suitable for producing the various crops may be found in every portion of the State, at prices ranging, per acre, from five to one hundred dollars. An article published during the past spring in one of the Jacksonville papers asserts : " The price of land is lower in proportion to productive value, advantages of market and facilities for transportation, than in any Northern State. Good agricultural lands on old improved estates and contiguous to railroads and thoroughfares can be had for from $5 to $25 per acre ; wild lands from 70 cents to $10 ; choice hammock lands on the St. Johns river, contiguous to steamboat landings, can be had in small or large tracts at about $20, while the contiguous pine lands, eligibly located, are to be had at from $5 to $10.

Lands along the line of the Transit and Peninsular Railroads being as productive as any in the State, are, upon the whole, perhaps, the most desirable, while, as has been before mentioned, these roads are extending their lines much further to the South, stretching through the Indian River region upon the east and to Tampa upon the west. When these roads are completed lands will be open to immigration which for fertility and ease of transportation will be exceeded by none in the United States.

But Florida has advantages for others besides the immigrant and settler. For the capitalist there are railroads to be built, canals to be constructed, new districts to be opened up, lines of steamers to be started and banks to be founded. For the laborer or mechanic there is work here, there, everywhere. For the gentleman of leisure there is a winter paradise, where his gun and rod need never lie idle. For the sight-seer and tourist there is novelty, the object for which he seeks, and beauty, such as perhaps he has never seen before. For all men there all things, and no one except the man who makes his business that of shovelling snow will be una-to find employment in Florida.

APPENDIX.

———•———

Notes by George M. Barbour, Esq., on his Tour of Florida with Hon. Seth French, Commissioner for Immigration, 1882.

PAGE 14.—Florida has a soil in which can be grown every variety of fruit, flowers, garden vegetables, field crops or forest product, that grows in any temperate or semi-tropical region of the world. Every one has heard of its fabulous yields of oranges, lemons, and the like; and the stories told on this head are not always exaggerated. I have seen groves of oranges which produced from $200 to $4,000 the acre, and know of an acre of pine-apples that, within two years after the trees were cleared from its surface, yielded the owners (two bright young New York lads) $1,800.

I have seen fields of *wheat* ripening in January that produced 28 bushels to the acre; *corn* that produced in the same month 70 bushels to the acre.

Sugar cane that yielded $160, net profit, to the acre.

Irish potatoes producing 200 bushels to the acre.

Rice that paid a net profit of $200 the acre; and

Cassava that netted $150 per acre.

Watermelons and *garden vegetables* grow rapidly, attain great sizes, are of excellent quality, and, when convenient to city market or to lines of transportation, pay the producer from $100 to $1,000 per acre.

Of garden vegetables three and even four crops are sometimes taken from the same tract within 12 months.

THE SPRATT GROVE.

PAGE 38.—The Spratt grove is one of the finest in Florida, with 1000 orange trees growing on 10 acres. The founder came here about ten years ago, an old man, and with but little means or money. He commenced clearing the land all by himself, and now has a grove hard to surpass. The grove is sure to produce henceforth an income of several thousand dollars annually.

PAGE 42.—The grove owned by Major Norris had 11,000 trees, mostly on hammock lands, which are nearly all bearing; in fact he gathered last winter upwards of 460,000 oranges, filling 3,100 boxes. In time that grove will produce millions, yielding a princely revenue.

PAGE 51.—The grove of Col. J. W. Marshall, who came here from South Carolina after the war, now in full bearing, has been sold for $28,000 cash.

Notes of the same on a trip with Capt. Samuel Tanbanks, on an official pilgrimage through the Northern Section of the State in March.

Mr. N. C. Rippy has written a letter to the Tallahassee Floridian, containing information of value to immigrants.

Suwanee County. The pine lands produce about 15 bushels of corn per acre. A little manure and good cultivation will yield more than double that. Cotton, about a bale to two acres, sometimes three. Upland rice, 40 to 60 bushels per acre. Sugar cane does well and is a very profitable crop.

Turpentining has become quite an industry and there are several large tupentine farms in the county that are reported to be very profitable.

INDIAN RIVER REGION.

PAGES 138-9.—The pine lands largely predominate, some of very fair productive quality. There are also fine bodies of the most splendid hammocks peculiarly adapted to the growth of tropical fruits, orange, lemon, lime, citron, banana, plantain, pine-apple, guava, pomegranate, tamarind, sapodilla, avocado-pear, mamma-apple, sugar-apple, mango, papaw, cacao, date, cocoanut, pecan-nut, yam, ginger, casava, etc.

The orange is the leading crop. It requires three years from transplanting to commence bearing, then pays $100 per acre and soon runs to thousands. There have been $4,000 to $6,000 realized per acre in one season.

Bananas grow considerably north of this and pay from $1,200 to $2,000 per acre.

Pine-apples from $800 to $1,200 per acre.

Sugar cane grows astonishingly, attaining a height of 12 to 16 feet, single stalks yielding more than a gallon of juice, which, being boiled down, makes over a quart of thick syrup and produces 500 to 600 gallons of syrup per acre.

Of peas and pumpkins two crops from the same vine are raised in abundance, and potatoes flourish the year round.

PAGE 140.—With the proper railroad connections the Indian river region must come into repute for vegetables. It can supply even New York in the months of January, February and March with the most delicate varieties of tomatoes, peas, beans, green corn, cabbages, melons, etc.

PAGE 148.—*Gulf Coast.* All the land in the vicinity is good, and crops of everything that can be produced elsewhere in the semi-tropical portions of Florida will grow there and produce abundantly. The scenery is beautiful, the climate is wonderfully bland and equable, and game, fish, oysters, turtles, and the like, are found in inexhaustible quantities.

THE SANFORD GRANT AND ORANGE COUNTY.

PAGE 155.—The tract embraces 22 square miles, nearly all of good quality and susceptible of profitable cultivation. Everything, except the characteristically tropical fruits, thrives exceedingly well here, especially oranges, lemons, grapes, and garden vegetables. The famous Speer grove contains 550 trees standing on less than six acres of land. The trees are about 35 years old and yield annually from 400,000 to 500,000 oranges. Upwards of 600,000 have been gathered in specially favorable seasons. The crop of the season of 1880–1 was sold on the trees at $17 the 1000, and netted the owner upward of $6,800.

PAGE 159.—Indian corn, sugar cane, cotton, tobacco, rice, strawberries, cabbages, tomatoes, watermelons, and all garden products yield immense crops in the soil around Sanford. From one garden comprising three-quarters of an acre of land, four crops had been taken during the preceding twelve months by using a moderate amount of fertilizer. Think of that—*four crops in one year !*

In a report of Mayor Marks and the Hon. John G. Sinclair it is mentioned:

"Much valuable land is now open to the actual settler and may be had by others from government price at points remote from transportation, to $5, $10, $20, $30 and up to $100 or more per acre at points immediately on the railroad or lakes connecting with the rail."

PRICES OF LAND, CLEARING, ETC.

PAGE 244.—There is still much land to be had at the government price, but these are rarely so situated in respect to transportation facilities that it is wise to put an orange grove upon them. The price of land held for sale by private parties ranges from $5 to $125 per acre, the difference being due mainly to greater or less nearness to settlements or to lines of transportation.

The cost of clearing pine land is from $10 to $30 per acre, according to the amount of undergrowth and the amount of "grubbing" required. Of clearing hammock lands from $30 to $100 per acre.

The cost of plowing is from $3 to $5 per acre.

PAGE 297.—*Capital.* Money can be loaned on perfectly good security at from 10 to 18 per cent. per annum.

.

THE FAVORITE ROUTE FROM EUROPE

To the Fertile and Wealthy State of

FLORIDA,

(United States of America)

IS VIA.

ROTTERDAM (HOLLAND) TO NEW YORK,

AND THENCE TO

FERNANDINA.

The First-class Clyde Built Iron Steamships of the

Netherlands American Steam Navigation Company,

AMSTERDAM,	ROTTERDAM,
SCHIEDAM,	W. A. SCHOLTEN,
ZAANDAM,	P. CALAND,
EDAM,	LEERDAM, MAAS,

Having unsurpassed accommodation for Cabin and Steerage Passengers, leave

ROTTERDAM AND AMSTERDAM, ALTERNATELY,

Every week, on Saturday,

FOR NEW YORK,

From which latter port the passage to

FERNANDINA, FLORIDA,

Is made in THREE days by the Superior Steamers of the

MALLORY LINE.

RATES OF PASSAGE

FROM

ROTTERDAM, } TO FERNANDINA, FLORIDA,
AMSTERDAM, }

CABIN, $90 ; STEERAGE, $35.

For further information apply to

The Netherlands American Steam Navigation Company,

Rotterdam (Holland).

H. CAZAUX, General Agent,
27 South William Street, New York.

Or to WILLIAM H. MARTIN,
Florida Land Agent, 50 Broadway, New York.

Printed in the USA
CPSIA information can be obtained
at www.ICGtesting.com
LVHW051507271124
797559LV00011B/911

9781022733763